# Rooster

GERRY MCGRATH was born and raised in Helensburgh, Scotland. He is a graduate of Strathclyde University and worked for several years as a teacher of modern languages. His first collection of poetry *A to B* (Carcanet) was published in 2008. In 2004 he was a winner of the Robert Louis Stevenson Memorial Award and in 2007 received a New Writer's Bursary from the Scottish Arts Council. His poetry was included in the anthology *New Poetries IV* (Carcanet, 2007). He lives in North Ayrshire with his wife, Kate, and two sons, Liam and Owen.

GERRY McGRATH

*Rooster*

CARCANET

First published in Great Britain in 2012 by
Carcanet Press Limited
Alliance House
Cross Street
Manchester M2 7AQ

Excerpt from 'To Apollo' is from Zbigniew Herbert: *The Collected Poems
1956–1998*, translated by Alyssa Valles. Published by Ecco, 2007. Reprinted by
kind permission of HarperCollins Publishers.

Excerpt from 'A Pastoral' is from *The Veiled Suite: The Collected Poems of Agha
Shahid Ali*. Published by W.W. Norton & Company, Inc., 2009. Reprinted by
kind permission of W.W. Norton & Company, Inc.

Excerpt from 'Preludes' is from Tomas Tranströmer: *New Collected Poems*,
translated by Robin Fulton. Published by Bloodaxe Books Ltd, 2002. Reprinted
by kind permission.

Excerpt from 'Persephone' is from *Without End: New and Selected Poems* by
Adam Zagajewski, translated by several translators. Copyright © 2002 by
Adam Zagajewski. Translation copyright © 2002 by Farrar, Strauss and Giroux,
LLC. Reprinted by permission of Farrar, Strauss and Giroux, LLC.

Lines from 'Marina Tsvetaeva' are from *Dancing in Odessa* by Ilya Kaminsky,
published by Tupelo Press. Copyright © 2004 Ilya Kaminsky.
Used with permission.

Excerpt from 'A man-eating knife' is from *I Have Lots of Heart: Miguel Hernández,
Selected Poems*, translated by Don Share. Published by Bloodaxe Books Ltd, 1997.
Reprinted by kind permission of Bloodaxe Books Ltd, and the translator.

A CIP catalogue record for this book is available from the British Library
ISBN 978 1 84777 116 2
The publisher acknowledges financial assistance from Arts Council England

Supported by
**ARTS COUNCIL
ENGLAND**

Typeset by XL Publishing Services, Tiverton
Printed and bound in England by SRP Ltd, Exeter

To Liam

# Acknowledgements

I would like to thank the Scottish Arts Council for the award of a New Writer's Bursary, which helped to make this book possible.

I am very grateful to Krista McCullough, who very graciously granted permission to reproduce her photograph on the cover.

Thanks are due, too, to David Kinloch for his friendship, kindness and support.

And, of course, Kate, whose love matters most.

# Contents

## I

# I

*I am seeking a statue*
*Drowned in my youth*

Zbigniew Herbert

## Intimate Expanses

Expecting little to come
from the tired liturgy
of dreams
he tugged gently at the quilt
and kissed an ear
tasting on his lips while
she lay sleeping
an intimate expanse of skin.

# Snow

He looked out.
Snow was falling
with a certain pride
and fur-thick
like dead letters returning
without courtesy or love
from an eternal lamentable
office of shadows.

## White Sail

5 a.m.
Lying awake

I reach for you
sleeping

touch
the white sail

of your skin.

## The Opposite of Goodbye

Listen to the wife
of the expert in elegies
as she delivers
this from her husband

*Walk*
         *Dream*
*Love*

(as she reads)

*Friends*
*my happiness is nothing*
*without you*

## Only Light

Stay there while I go out
itchy with the stars
to feel blind for the inkwell

I know but I don't know

what every night allows me
why every day brings only light

# The Telling

The big square light and the smaller
rectangular light they see
through the steamed-up kitchen
window.
Not long now.
Cauliflower's taking a fork.
Turnip chips need just
a few minutes more in the oven.
The cheese sauce in a pot
bubbles occasionally
on the back of the hob.
Tonight he'll tell his wife
the story of a young girl
working up to telling her father
that he is going to be a grandfather
and him replying
aye daughter
I feel like a grandfather.

## St Petersburg

They drink tea
in St Petersburg

remembering conversations
about truth

and if not truth
the desire for truth

and if not desire

# Element

The sea –
a sweet, blue history
of the Earth.

Gravity –
the soil's otherness,
pulse of the crowd felt
in an empty room.

## The Beach at Irvine

The seal disdains the rocks
to follow the express
lift shaft
down.

Up-periscopes
when it hears the fanfare
of the stage designers arriving
from olive-green dreams.

## The Photographer

We see things
you and I –

orange beech leaves

hills

the skin of a pool

a lighthouse beam

of frost

## Pale Cup

A blue light

you breathing the impossible
flowers under snow.

*

Rain crossed the glass.
Light bloomed
in the pale cup of the room.
Sadness was banished
by the briefest gift
of words.

# No Maybes About It

*For Pedro Lenz*

He was sure
he'd seen it
or heard it
or both
:
poetry should be
the linguistic equivalent
of lemon juice
—

aye and no

## You Are

Peel me away You are
my love
my not-death

emptiness cupped
between the light heart
the starry bone

You are    whispers
where the facts cry out
and silence reigns.

## Lightning

Everything I wanted to say
to the hard-hearted women
the forsaken children.

How much dearer to them
in a sea-green afternoon
the memory of a morning
made giddy by the lightning
speed of the past.

# Changed Days

Outside, on the pavement, a cool breeze
administered its soothing balm.
Inside, a decayed tooth had been salved
by the expeditionary skill of a dentist
who never claimed the subtlety of the tongue
which, hours later, all numbness gone,
began the process of mapping this familiar
unfamiliar terrain.

## The Guests

The conduit for laughter.
The conduit for eternal laughter.

Swallows flit in and out
through the dark-eyed ruin.

When evening puts out the light
the skin of the earth remains
lighter than air.

I have to tell you:
there's been no word
of tomorrow.

But at least I can tell you,
I who have been so long away,
you who are only just arriving.

## Summer's End

is a hill
bleared by rain

a first trembling
wind

the memory
that into autumn's room
winter will dip a glass

hold up darkness
to a chittering lantern
moon.

# First

The consensus is you are reading
or were that day
the camera snapped you

in your half-world, a mothy flicker
evoking open-mouthed wonder in ours.

Whisper it through the walls, wee yin,
we have forgotten

the secrets heard
when gravity first pulls
on the silvery shadow.

# Blue Box

Ancestors, what did you find out?
Life's short. Nothing can be added
or taken away.
Joy isn't just hope without the dog-hair
of despair.
Adjectives always ride piggyback.

We know you're there because we feel you,
Ghosts' bones.

Ten thousand years ago the sky was
a blue box above your head,
the moon was the socket for an eye,
the stars faded quicker than the dying light

that grows.

## Open Wide

Dark winds buffet the house.
The air is wet as stone.
I am tired of forever.

Slowly daylight grows,
sweet calm awaits.
I throw my arms open wide.
Morning is here.

# Kisses

She asked me to do two things before leaving.
One was write a letter. Then she kissed me.
In town, I slipped her letter into the post box, heard it fall.
Across the street a man had stopped with his dog.
Everywhere people were running from the rain.

# Loose Ends

*For Czeslaw Milosz*

I read a short poem
that takes some forgiving.
He is gone now.

My father drifts to mind
grey face leaking hope
that all the loose ends
will be gathered in.

## Wheat

I want you to listen, to think of a field
yellow with wheat.
Please, cast no aspersions, envy no one,
remember nothing, not even yourself.

## Magic

He spent years thinking
how he wished never to see
the word on the page
hear its opposing voice
nor think of the space it is given.
Then suddenly Yes's Opposite
conjuring all manner of things
as if by magic a future.

## He Says

They sit in the dry reservoir
of their front room.
She laughs, cries, whispers.
Memory is everything.
*How can I tell you I love you?*
Somewhere it is raining.

## In Itself

Who needs the genius of diffident earth,
the inborn rhythm of toppled coins.
I am closer to you than a pen to paper,
an itch to skin. Love is unthinkable.
Age, an insufficiency in itself.

## La Stanza Rossa

Red is the room
brown the chair
blue the vase
green the tree

that burns

# Born

With the announcement
of the death of irony
a strange new world is born.

Doors toll on their hinges.
Shadows dark as eyelashes
silence the wild flowers.

Trees stick two fingers up
at the blue-bottomed boat.

Beside a cricket pitch
a conference of crows is helpless
with laughter.

# Fragment (of a Chorale)

*For David Kinloch*

Darkness
Plump as a pigeon

Daybreak
Deft, putty-white

Urgency
In a dew drop

# Eldest

On the days that time sleeps
she dreams of last kisses.

*Terrible things will die with me*

He listens, then takes his leave
beating his wings like a bird.

# Blue

Try to love
live your life

as if dreaming
believing truth
is nothing if not
forgettable.

Tonight the air is blue
under rain.

# Roses

This heart lacking
no pain
or human statistic
carries roses
to the far corners of a rock
tilted at the sun.

## Two Words

Like a look, like a light, they come
arrows in the blood fleeing a fire.

You could say the waterfall began the day
death in something like his father's jacket,
smiling that tender, angular smile, stepped
off the bus and walked to the foot of the road.

# Report from a West Highland Funeral

Last Saturday at three o'clock in the afternoon
adrenalin with a clatter of hooves
burst from the walls of the piss-poor hotel lounge.

Slave to reason
I remained in my seat.

# I Hope

Poetry – heart's vice!
Your future lies
where lyric and environmental
concerns are intimates.

In my son's blue gaze
a terrible clarity confers grace
while honesty like a vulture
circles overhead.

I hope
no man finds this verse lethal.

## You Were

This Friday afternoon
after the coffee I didn't want
I decide

I've had enough of playing daddy
to your wide-eyed baby boy.

One day
time will uproot itself
shake the dirt from its shoes
show us the cuts on its hands
its legs
say to us, father and son

you were more beautiful
when you didn't know you were.

## Tell Me

what you want
from me

with these few words

this cool approximation
of honey

after a long hard century
of doubt.

## Ask

In a blind conceit
they queue

the slow river
swans ducklings
the summer on gigantic feet

So I ask
if the present is sadness
what is the past

# Standing

Undressing, she points at the whirligig
sedate in the backyard. Pineapple
scent of mayweed lingers on her fingers.
Harvest moon climbs through the cherry tree.

Look at it now, she says.

Later
standing by the upstairs window
naked
in a dim light

## Script

Yes
the future lies somewhere

in the unclasped pen
in the brick

the spider altars

in the ash potency
of your script.

It is nowhere
you are.

## Zero

Singly
the heart limns
unwritables:

wind turbines
hay bales
the endless return of a wheel

to zero.

## Steps

Fearless
you step on tiny feet
among crocodiles
mega *bloks*
unbuttoned books

look along your nose
at the dragon traffic
the three-legged cat

the clumsy tree
shedding ghosts.

## Moon

Come as you please, with a hunchback's
knowledge, as white cloud escaping
from a slender pot, as a dappled lawn,
I will pray for you

remembering with a kind of blood-excitement
laughter, a rapt chamber, your cool hand
pressed to the moon's warm flank.

# II

*We'll tear our shirts for tourniquets
and bind the open thorns, warm the ivy
into roses*

Agha Shahid Ali

# Goat Fell

One thing's clear; I knew you when
you had the eye of a horse, wore a livery
of blue snow and cemetery thistle
before you shrank to a grain of sand.
Now mountain, turquoise river, lilac haze
you would age us.

## Audience of One

Forget the poet losing himself
in a blue beard of words. Somewhere
I have your picture, wall-less, nail-less,
string-less, just you immeasurably,
an audience of one.

## Imperfect

Tarkovsky picks up
the drumsticks of his art
shoots his darkest
dream –
        what the colour blue means
        to a man woken at four
        by a child

        an imperfect life.

# Suite No. 1

For Margareta Persson

*Two truths draw nearer each other.*
*One comes from inside, one comes*
*from outside. Where they meet*
*we have a chance to see ourselves.*

Tomas Tranströmer

## Wordleft

Who, what are you listening to
closed, hard up to the frost
in air that was made for you.
Or so I thought. Now

I see with a painter's eye
the tea horizon, soot, cauliflower white,
the raw pigment of your rage –

cadmium deep orange
quinacridone red
umber.

Here is a space for living,
the paint-layered grain
where silence speaks to break
its wordleft divinity.

Here are your words at swim
in the fond sea metaphor,
breathing the terrible moth-kiss
breath of hope.

Now those colours are precise.
Prime, indivisible, they complete
the picture. It is a kind of triumph
to see things as they are; exacting lines,
an organisation of space, the *blend*
of passivity. And all the while
an echo of uncertainty keeps us ill at ease,
magnifies, approaches.


*Spheres*

The dwelling is finished.
Perhaps adorn the anteroom.
Hang it with portraits…

★

What's missing isn't there
hysterically.

Irony's infectious.
For example,

'Why dark green?'
Why? Paint crowds
the corners
where Time leaks.

★

You sigh because
you share that compassion
for all objects

laughter
writes its name
on the limpid spheres
surrounding them.


## Two Rivers

Nothing, then later in life, a tidal discovery.
Water is transformational. The weft and wap
of a burn's animal spine, stones as metric eggs,
the punctilious grass just here and no further.
See, square after square, the picture builds.
No matter. We drink from two rivers. You wait
but you also forget waiting.


## Silence Cut

From this distance there's only
rumour and hearsay
that you don't paint farewells,
a faint, diminutive trickle
of half-words
telling us that outright vanishings
are impossible.

Something's happened since yesterday.
A white canvas was briefly on display.
Now there's a little symmetry and an unquiet
reddish wash.
At the exhibition people admired the diptych.
Privately they talked of little else.

# III

*Persephone goes underground again*
*and again the same thread of indifference*
*binds my tiny bird-heart.*

Adam Zagajewski

# Wave

Like a patient awaiting surgery
the car sits by the roadside, bonnet up.
Outside it's dark as June.
With a wave of the hand she declines.

*I try not to make the same mistake twice*

Something like that.

# A Man of Good Fortune

There is no cabin, no ship,
no native land to quit.
Just poppies born of silence
spilling on the far bank.

What do I call you
who share the stillness with me
Whose echoes
on the thrumming air
whisper

*who will you see*
*what will you do*
*when I abandon you*

# The Morning of Forgetfulness

Old grey men and the easy money
buried in the folds of your snout,
you look up as if expecting
what might fall –

So I take a painting in the shape
of a bowl of water and let you drink
from the morning of forgetfulness

when everything has been observed,
like the dark river, cattle grazing,
a face, it too deeply furrowed.

# Dutch Interiors

My Dear, the room is very small.
The wardrobe's filled with my clothes.
My suitcase sits on its end, slightly open.
From the corner of an eye I see a hand
holding a jug from which trickles nightly
a braid of milk.

# Faith

Tired of forever
he pictures nothing
when they sing,
no odourless quantity,
tributary of sound
ghosting from the stairs
where a boyish shadow
blindly keeps the faith.

# IV

*All I want is a human window*
*in a house whose roof is my life*

Ilya Kaminsky

# Return to the City

The world was differently lit.
We lived with the dregs of sweetness,
a cracked voice announcing our old age.
Unable to stand still you dug deeper
until from the abandoned barracks
silence spoke: I don't remember, it said,
palm trees swaying, a river flowing quietly
through its heart.

# Foreign Travel

      … in airport foyers
where light travels in its summer dress,
kissing their families, kissing the air
around their families goodbye:
how quietly the wolf.
In four hours darkness will fall
over the splintered roof
where a girl who prayed nightly
into clasped hands
          died in her sleep.

## Rooster

            rain falls overnight,
a river flows gull-grey, roseate, burning:
the desire to be silent, still, to live
outside the body, praising the dead.

     who loves the sound of the rooster
tearing at the day
            will be killed for his blood.

## Suite No. 2

### I

Frost returns like a dog
to lay the stick at his feet:
the day ripens to music.

Snowdrops
       lilac sky
              blackbird's soft

cantilena

what returns your trembling
sweetness?

### II

Under sifting rain the finches
steadfastly at the feeder;
he readies the secateurs,
pushes back the hawthorn
to reveal cobwebs
spun around its heart.

### III

In that milky delirium
a needle scratching
endlessly under the lid.
Today they discharge you
from the heights
to walk the crazy bird-walk,
dark ribbons
flapping at your wing.

## IV

  September
memory of mornings
scribed in a snail's arabesque.
He sits up: *el ultimo suspiro*.
Keep your secrets like a child's,
in the leafless book. Youth
and a thousand years of history
can pass in an afternoon.


## V

In the darkness
muffled sounds, like fruit
falling from a tree.


## VI

Poetry of the high altitudes,
the earth's blue breath:
seconds before oblivion
the icy hand of a stranger.


## VII

The meagre beam of a bridge
idling in the half-light,
connecting this island to that.

The need for speeches is past.
Gleaming in the high buttonhole
a winter rose.

# VIII

No tender insignia on the bluish mesh.
Dust blows from the honeycombs.
The city burns like a candle at noon.
Out of the mist a swan's flight hands him
                                    to the light.

# V

*Where can I be*
*that I will not find loss?*

Miguel Hernández

# West Coast Colloquy

Bladderwrack: Prostrate, moribund, you are bound by the laws of primitive gases, and the added distraction of the rats that feed and shit in your hair.

Coal ship: The cackled go-ahead to crank through the rucked greyness, creep along the island's jaw, the engine's *pompe funèbre* for company, snow on the mountains. The frozen waterfalls will shortly sigh, unburdened.

Crab: Look up from the mall at the presidential plush. The day evolves. Dog Star shining down gilds the environs you call home. Rockpool caudillo, you have company. Around a speck of dust an oyster is wrapping its soft armature. Life accrues, turns tough; the dead-eyed pearl.

Dead Letter: I am on a balcony, somewhere hot. My fingers smell of cordite. A book is falling apart in my hands; leaves me with stitches. The bougainvillea is lovely. When I think of you a small red cup changes hands.

Coastal Path: I keep you in my pocket, indecent, a whimsy for when the white rhymes are unremarkable. Then you slip out, genie-like, down the modest promenade, the long-fingered walk, to crouch in the kelp where you nod at the mountain palette like you're counting the cones on a fir.

Arran: What is your ambit, Island? How far your reach? You have seen enough to make the Deity's bean counter blush; looked on at children playing bassoons at earthworms to prove an ancient point. And yet, on a failed evening, I have seen you bandaged; a smear of snow and the indrawn starlight. My dreams are an open book, briefly held: the blink of a horse, blessed provinces, the poetry of yes, the needle of a compass quivering to a point.

Shape up, it's time to slip
from darkness
to the green-eyed world,
each step
an act of brinkmanship,
first one claw foot
then the other.

Lickety-split, griffon,
slay elephants, breathe flame.
If down the apartment door
a talon drags,
a lion's paw will rise up,
snuff out your fire
and things will never be
the same.

## Horse Feathers

From outside a ripple of applause; good shot
or a concert's end. Perhaps the king is dead
and these rooks are his po-faced children
medalled up in pawnbroker's velour.

On the roof opposite a parish council of gulls
is discussing matters raised: was the Finnish
curmudgeon right? In the thousand-mile garden
a deciduous silence quiets the starlings' shout.

Can we learn from exile's glacial light?
Or does the end arrive in the sculptor's glance,
his blade?

# *Purple*

Etched
on the Lebanese cedar:
*punicus*, southern vintage, a calf's liver.

Porphyry,
what your colour hides:
born a king
and in a painted field
died.